This Journal Belongs To

● ●

I0706876

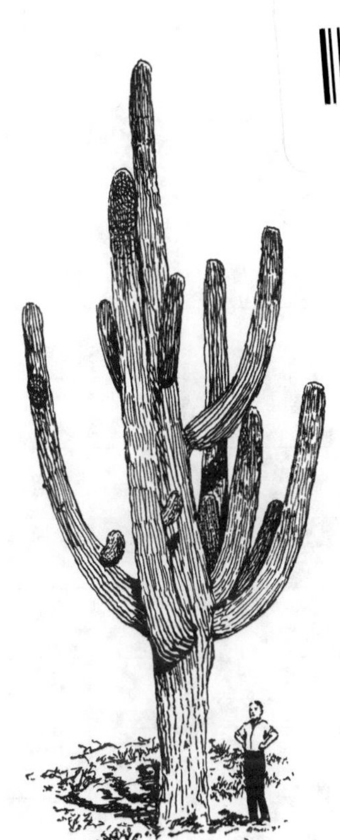

Cactus Related Gifts For Teen Man Women Sister Nurse Kids Girl Or Teens 120 Pages

All Rights Reserved By Aivaras Kovaliukas

Designed by pikisuperstar / Freepik